MW00873169

M is for Majestic

Barbara Rasco

ISBN:
ISBN-13:9781723974687

DEDICATION

This book is lovingly dedicated to my husband of 41 years…and counting. Billy, you are greatly loved and truly my very best friend. Thank you, sweetheart, for spending hundreds of hours chauffeuring me thousands of miles across Wyoming's highways, back roads, up and down mountain switchbacks, and narrow treacherous dirt roads in search of breath-taking scenery and amazing critters to photograph. We've had to ask help to get us out of snow drifts, paid tow trucks to pull us out of the mud. We've had to leave the truck in grizzly country and hike and loudly pray our way to safety. We've driven in white-out conditions, pouring rain and the brightest of sunshine. Some trips more successful than others. Every trip an adventure! I love you, and I love the life that we share together. How very blessed are we!

Agile

A is for Agile

The agile deer makes it look easy to leap over a fence.

Did you know that a white tail deer has the capability to jump 15 feet high!

How high can you jump?

Bashful

B is for Bashful

Can you find the bashful deer hiding behind the tree? What gives her away?

Did you know that the average span between a mature mule deer buck's ears is 20 inches to 22 inches from tip to tip?

Are you bashful or bold?

Clever

C is for Clever

Look at this very clever bison! He chose to lead the others to leap over the lowest beam in the fence.

Did you know that the massive bison can jump up to six feet!

Can you think of a time when your idea made doing something easier?

Dappled

D is for Dappled

Look at these darling dappled fawns as they pose with their mother for the picture!

Did you know that the spots on the fawns help to camouflage them and keep them safe?

A warm coat helps to keep you safe during frigid winter days. Can you name another item of clothing that will protect you from the weather?

Exquisite

E is for Exquisite

The exquisite dragonfly looks as if it is made of fine-spun gold.

Did you know that dragonflies eat other insects, including those pesky mosquitoes and gnats!

What insect do you think is most beautiful?

Frisky

F is for Frisky

After running around the big rocks, it looks as if this frisky chipmunk stopped to take a moment to smell the bright yellow dandelion.

Did you know that like the enormous grizzly bear, chipmunks also hibernate in dens during the winter months?

Do you like to run and play outside when you have a lot of energy?

Graceful

G is for Graceful

The graceful swan is enjoying a peaceful swim across the lake.

Did you know that the trumpeter swan is the largest of the waterfowl family, and they can live for over 20 years?

Have you ever seen a clumsy animal that made you laugh?

Healthy

H is for Healthy

The healthy marmot is munching on fresh green grass for his lunch.

Did you know that the marmot sometimes communicates by making a whistling sound? That's why they are sometimes called whistle pigs.

Eating fresh fruits and vegetables helps us grow healthy bodies. What is your favorite healthy food to eat?

Inquisitive

I is for Inquisitive

The inquisitive grizzly bear cub stood up to see the crowd that was gathering to take his picture.

Did you know that grizzly bear cubs will generally stay with their very protective mothers until they are 3 years old?

Are you curious about things? What would be an excellent job for a person who likes to ask questions?

Jovial

J is for Jovial

This jovial prairie dog family looks like they are taking a fun ride on a roller-coaster.

Prairie dogs are very social little critters. They are close relatives to chipmunks and marmots, not dogs like their name suggests.

What is your favorite thing to do as a family?

Keen

K is for Keen

The keen wolf will use his extreme hearing and sense of smell to hunt for food.

Did you know that wolf pups are born deaf and blind?

What is your favorite smell?

Lofty

L is for Lofty

The lofty bald eagle, soaring high in the blue sky, is a beautiful symbol of courage and freedom.

Did you know that bald eagles aren't really bald? They are called bald eagles because of the white feathers that cover their heads.

If you could fly like an eagle, where would you go?

Majestic

M is for Majestic

The majestic bighorn sheep confidently climb along the rocks and crags high in the Rocky Mountains.

Did you know that the massive curled horns on a mature ram can weigh up to 30 pounds? Another fact: the pupils in their eyes are horizontal giving them over 300 degrees in their field of vision; easier to spot predators!

What is the grandest animal you have ever seen?

Nurturing

N is for Nurturing

The nurturing mama bison cares for her calf.

Did you know that all bison calves are born with a reddish-brown color? Calves are able to stand a short time after they are born.

Can you name different ways to care for a pet?

Observant

O is for Observant

The observant red-tailed hawk is able to see a small mouse from 100 feet in the air.

Did you know that red-tailed hawks like to hunt for their food high from tree tops or telephone poles?

Are you an observant person? Do you easily notice the little things around you?

Powerful

P is for Powerful

It is very smart and important to remain a safe distance from the very powerful bison.

Did you know that the American bison (also referred to as buffalo) is the largest North American land animal? The bull can weigh up to 2000 pounds and can run up to speeds of 35 miles per hour!

How fast do you think you can run?

Quirky

Q is for Quirky

The quirky face of a moose is almost cartoon-like.

Not only does the moose have a very long face, but did you know that its muzzle can droop over its chin?

Can you make a silly face?

Radiant

R is for Radiant

The radiant wings of the swallowtail butterfly are so vivid in the bright sunshine.

Did you know that there are over 500 species of swallowtail butterflies? They also come in a vast variety of beautiful colors. And, they taste with their feet!

Some people think yellow is a happy color. What color makes you happy?

Sparring

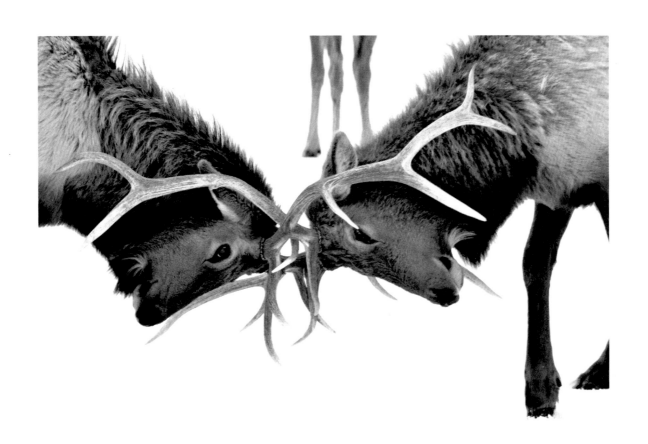

S is for Sparring

The sparring bull elk practice and show off their strength on a chilly winter day.

Did you know that the high-pitched sound that the bull elk makes is called bugling?

There's a saying, "practice makes perfect." Is there something that you practice every day to help you improve ?

Twin

T is for Twin

The twin pronghorn calves remain very close to their mother. Do you think their mother can tell them apart?

Did you know that the pronghorn (commonly referred to as antelope) is the fastest land animal in the western hemisphere? They can run up to 60 miles per hour!

Can you name two identical items in your house?

Untamed

U is for Untamed

The untamed horse represents the spirit of the west.

Did you know that untamed horses can be very dangerous?

If you could name a wild horse, what would it be?

Vocal

V is for Vocal

Early in the morning and late in the evening, the very vocal meadowlark's sweet song can be heard across the prairie.

Did you know that the western meadowlark is the state bird of six states? (Montana, Kansas, Nebraska, North Dakota, Oregon and Wyoming)

What is your favorite song to sing?

Whimsical

W is for Whimsical

The whimsical black bear cubs play under the watchful eye of their mother.

Did you know that the long sharp claws on black bears allow them to be great tree climbers? When the cubs are high up in a tree they are safe from predators.

Do you have a favorite game that you like to play with your friends?

Xilinous

X is for Xilinous

The xilinous cottontail bunny looks so furry and soft.

Did you know that cottontail rabbits get their name because their tails look like a white piece of cotton?

Can you name other things that are soft like cotton? If cotton is soft and wood is hard, do you think a cottonwood tree would feel soft or hard?

Young

Y is for Young

The young mountain bluebirds are hungrily waiting for their parents to feed them.

Did you know that the main diet of the mountain bluebird is insects?

What is your favorite snack?

Zealous

Z is for Zealous

The zealous fox remains focused on its prey.

Did you know that foxes don't live in packs like their relatives the wolves? For the most part, the fox is a solitary animal; they hunt and sleep alone.

Is it easy for you to stay focused on a task, or do you tend to daydream?

Acknowledgments

I'd like to acknowledge our amazing God, our Creator and Sustainer of life; the One who spoke all the beauty that surrounds me into existence. Thank you, Lord, for giving me the means and the passion to enjoy Your creation to the fullest. How I love to see in the distance, beyond my deck and little patch of Wyoming, the beautiful Wind River Mountain Range. I have so much fun thinking about all the critters, large and small, that call those magnificent mountains home. I hope I never take my view for granted.

I'd like to acknowledge my mom, Darla Hapgood, and my youngest sister, Allison Pittman. While visiting our 98-year-old Grandma in a Las Cruces, New Mexico hospice, Allison and Mom quietly collaborated and came up with the idea for *me* to write this book. Oh! how Grandma loved her many decades of Wyoming life! I can't help but wonder if she secretly heard the soft tones of your voices and went back to sweet times. Thank you, both, for your confidence in my simple abilities, and for your help with editing! Oh, Allison, you're so right, it's hard to edit your own work!

I'd like to also acknowledge Dee Hapgood. Thank you, Daddy, for opening the many e-mailed files, making it easier for Mom to see and read every changed manuscript, in its entirety!

27736690R10036

Made in the USA
Lexington, KY
03 January 2019